Be Kind

Fulton Books
Meadville, PA

Published by Fulton Books 2023

ISBN 979-8-88505-551-2 (paperback)
ISBN 979-8-88505-552-9 (digital)

Printed in the United States of America

Be Kind

For Mary Aileen Mooney

EILEEN TEEL

One day, Patrick was
playing with his truck.

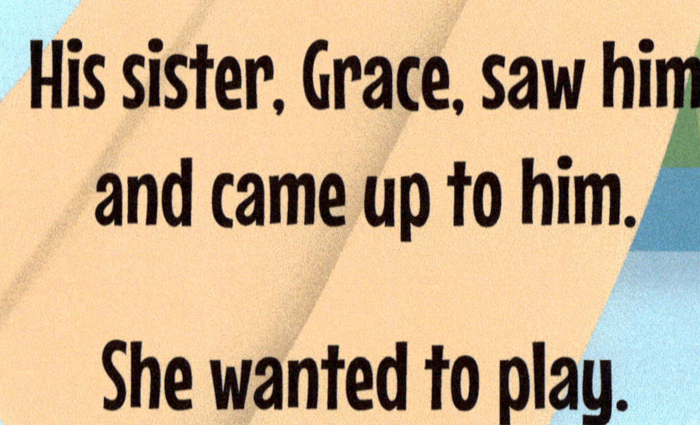

His sister, Grace, saw him
and came up to him.

She wanted to play.

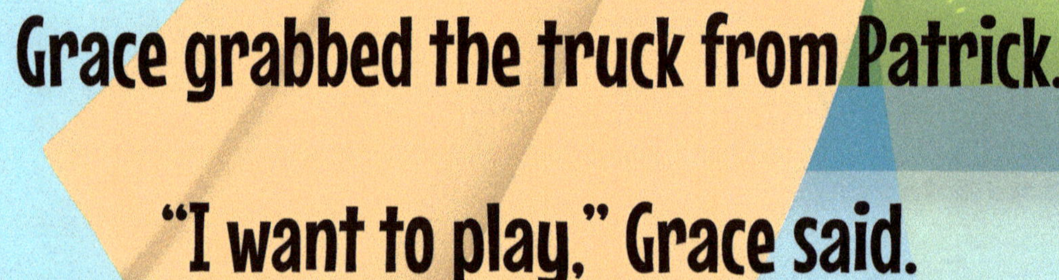

Grace grabbed the truck from Patrick.

"I want to play," Grace said.

Patrick grabbed the truck and said, "No, I had it first!"

Grace cried. Her feelings were hurt.

Mom was watching from across the room and said to Grace, "If you want to play with the truck, you might want to ask your brother if you can, don't just grab it from him, *be kind.*"

Grace looked at her brother
and asked, "Can I please
play with your truck?"

TOYS

Thinking of what his mother just told his sister, *be kind*, Patrick handed the truck to Grace.

TOYS

The mother was so proud of her children that she packed a picnic of snacks, and they all sat on a blanket in the living room and talked about their day.

Be kind.

18

The next morning, Grace
went to school.

She loves to walk to the
bus with her friends.

It was a beautiful sunny day, and
Grace was excited to see everyone.

As the day went on, Grace noticed
her friend Mary seemed sad.

Grace asked Mary, "What's
wrong? Are you sad?"

"I am sad," Mary said. I forgot my
favorite blanket for nap time.

"I'm sorry Mary," said Grace.

Grace went to her seat and thought about what her mother said when she was arguing with her brother... *Be kind.*

24

Grace thought, *Hey! I have an idea!*

Grace was so excited about her idea; she couldn't wait until recess to talk with Mary!

When recess time came, Grace and
Mary met on the playground.

Grace excitingly whispered, "Mary,
you can use my blanket for nap time!"

Mary's face lit up with a bright smile.

Mary said, "Thank you, Grace. You're
a good friend and very kind."

The two friends went back into
the classroom for a nice rest.
Grace proudly smiled to herself,
thinking, *I can't wait to tell Mom
what I did in school today!*

Be kind.